THE BOOK FOR THE TOTAL HEALTH OF THE SICK

Learn How To Stay Healthy And Live Longer

You Can Get Healed From That Sickness Tormenting Your Life

I AM THE
LORD
WHO
HEALS
YOU

Brave Mic, PhD

Scriptural quotes are from the New International Version (NIV) Holy Bible translation, unless otherwise stated. The *Slash* (/), where indicated, is used to differentiate writings from scripture quotations. The *'READ'*, where indicated, requires that the quotation where the write up has its footing. The first digit(s) of the Quotation usually followed by a column *(:)* for instance *John 3*: represents the Chapter of the book, while the digit(s) that follows after the column *(:)*, for instance *John 3:16*, represents the verse. A dash or hyphen *(-)* that follows after the verse digit(s), for instance *John 3:16-18*, shows that the verse is to be continued till the last number or digit(s) that ends the quotation.

Title of Book:	I AM THE LORD WHO HEALS YOU
Subtitle:	The Book For The Total Health Of The Sick
Category:	Health, Healing / Deliverance Series
Size:	5.83" x 8.27"
Original Author:	Dr. Brave Mic

Copy right © Brave Mic Publishing World, JUNE 21st, 2015. All rights reserved. This book or any portion thereof may not be reproduced or used in any manner whatsoever without the express written permission of the publisher except for the use of brief quotations in a book review.

Edition:	Second Edition
First Published:	July, 2017
ISBN:	9798790769450

Typeset and edited: Brave Mic

Contact the Author:
Founder & President
Salvation Miracles Embassy Inc.
Port Harcourt, Nigeria
M/Phone: +234 803 264 5496
eMail: pastorbravemic@gmail.com

This Book is Dedicated to

**His Excellency,
Alabo Tonye Graham
Douglas, OFR** (The Orubibi VI of Abonema Kingdom)   - The Hezekiah of our Time -

Content

Introduction   4-14

Chapter One: 15-36
The Roots Of Sicknesses

Chapter Two: 37- 85
Reasons You Are Sick

Chapter Three: 86-99
The Bruiser And the Healer

Chapter Four: 100-111
Look At the Brazing Serpent

Chapter Five: 112-150
Here Comes Your Healing

Chapter Six: 151-168
Now That You Are Well

Chapter Seven: 169-179
Get Saved And Live Happily

Read Other Books
By Brave Mic   180-188

Introduction

The passages in this book will be dealing with sicknesses and divine healing from God.

Sicknesses, as we know, are often seen as ailments, diseases, bad health, viruses, infections, vomiting, and bugs, and many more, which hampers on the human physical body. But sickness, from God's perspective goes beyond the general concept. In this book, God sees a sinner [someone who keeps doing what is against God's word] as a sick person. This means anyone living in sin is sick/ Read: Matthew 9:12-13.

And what is sin? It is the transgression [or violation,

misuse, and disregard] of the Law/ Read: 1ˢᵗ John 3:4. The Law itself is empowered by sin to prosecute violators/ Read: 1ˢᵗ Corinthians 15:56. This brings about various penalties like sicknesses to the wrong doers, making them groan and feel severe pains both on the body, spirit, soul, heart, and the general life respectively/ Read: Romans 2:12; 4:15.

Sicknesses on these sets of persons are often extended to their farmlands, businesses, marriages, family relatives, and other life ventures. Everything around them gets sick one way or the other/ Read: Malachi 3:8-12.

There is a worse kind of sickness this book will be emphasizing on, which is spiritual sickness. It is the loss of one's spiritual strength or the absence of salvation from the bondage of sin in a person's life. If a person is well all over and doesn't have salvation in Christ, such a person is spiritually sick.

Spiritual sickness is indeed the worse kind of sickness because the sick person has no hope of living or surviving at the afterlife.

Anyone who is separated from God is dead already even though he or she is alive in the physical world. This is why God is so much interested in your spiritual healing as well as your all round healing/ Read: 3rd John 2.

But not all sicknesses have their roots from sin. Sometimes God gives permission to the devil to inflict sicknesses on righteous people. He does this to test and to know those who truly belong to him. A biblical example of this kind of test is seen on the man called Job/ Read: Job 2:6-7.

In another plan, God also inflict sicknesses on righteous people to keep them from being proud. The apostle Paul is a typical example of this kind of test experience/ Read: 2nd Corinthians 12:7.

God inflict sicknesses on people to test them, refine them, and make them turn back from their evil ways; while Satan inflict sicknesses on people as an act of wickedness to mar their destinies, get them to curse God, separate them from their true worship, and destroy them completely. But God's purpose and plan also brings healing to the bruised. What is healing? It is the act or process of curing, giving remedy, and making well, all those who have been sick, including everything around them.

It is often very possible for professional medical doctors to cure ailments. They do it by trying out various medications both in a highly scientific practice and in the local laboratories. Medicines in form of tablets, syrups, pills, injections, as well as balms, all are produced from the mixtures or tried out drugs, approved for human health as well as the health of other domestic creatures. But in spite of all the medicines in the world, sick people taking these prescribed drugs still suffer unimproved health from the same illnesses. The fact is scientists are yet to or, still trying to find out or give solutions to such cases.

Most medical scientists have come to the understanding that aside professional research and contributions to human health, there is always a need to refer to the eminent divine power of healing. This means it is absolutely useless for human doctors to try to make a name when the big doctor – God, is always available to handle critical health cases.

In spite of these facts, many people have depended so much on drugs and strange sources of healing which comes from the devil rather than looking up to God, who both the source and cure of their perfect healing.

King Ahaziah is the man who consulted Baal-Zebub, the god of Ekron, seeking for recovery from his illness. But God was angry with him saying "…Is there no God (healing balm) in Israel?" And as a result he died in his sickness and never recovers/ Read 2nd Kings 1:2-4, 16-17.

With the spate of reoccurring outburst of pestilences and plagues in the world today, it is indeed clear evidence that God is in the move to heal and to rescue human dignity from bondage. There is a healing solution already in the world. When a source of healing is discovered, a sickness no longer has power over its victim. No doubts; God can minister healing through many ways even in the medicines prescribed by medical scientists.

To be on the safe side, it is very important that everyone come to know the roots of sicknesses, reasons why people get sick, who the bruiser and healer is, why look at the brazing serpent, when comes your healing, after you have gotten well, and the need to get saved and live happily. All these will be made clearer as you read this book.

This is the assurance for your healthy living: if only you will stop doing wrong today, but pray to him, and ask for forgiveness; then you will not suffer the diseases or sickness others are experiencing. Sin can give room for attack of sicknesses into your life. Once you become well again don't go back to sin/ Read: John 5:14.

There is the Doctor of doctors, and you need to recognize him. He is the LORD who heals you! He does what human doctors cannot do. He sends sicknesses on people who are often disobeying God's word by living evil lives/ Read: Exodus 15:26.

Are you or your family members presently suffering from an ailment? That is not a problem because God says, "...I am the Lord who heals you!" God's healing power works through medicines. Sometimes, too, he discards those drugs and heals right away. His healing hand is already position in your body now. But will you turn to him and be healed today?

This book will act as divine healing medicine for every reader. Each line and page has power to miraculously remove those illnesses and keeps one completely healed. Very important: the reader who takes time to read this book and believes in the power of healing from the LORD should expect instant healing from disappointment, heart break, depression, HIV / AIDS, arthritis, fever, diabetes, stroke, fear, regular flow of blood, abuse, cancer, barrenness, Ebola, PTSD, Covid-19, trauma, and many other sicknesses infecting the human health.

It begins by feeling sorry for one's wrong doings and turning back to God. This is the only way to be rest assured that healing is possible with his word: "...I am the LORD who heals you!"

Chapter 1: THE ROOTS OF SICKNESSES

The root to every sickness is sin, and a person living in sin is sick/ Read: Matthew 9:12-13. Every sin you commit attracts a sickness and sometimes leads to many other sicknesses even natural death, unless there is intervention/ Read: 1st John 5:16-17.

Truth speaking, sin is like a cankerworm. It spreads into all parts of the body and destroys a person's health and life slowly. Whenever that one sickness or sin is not treated or purged out, it often leads to inventing many destructive others. But when you know the root or cause of a problem, then it is possible to find solution.

Sicknesses are not part of God's will for humans. It came from the misused of the law of God. Indeed sickness is one of the punishments God uses to inflict on disobedient people, and at the same time, refine righteous people. So whenever you break the natural laws of life, you are at that point open to the attack of any kind of sicknesses/ Read: Romans 7:10.

Prophet Habakkuk says that plagues go before him, and pestilence follows behind him/ Read: Habakkuk 3:5. This means that

God has in his entourage deadly sicknesses which he unleashes on people in the past, present, and future.

The book of Deuteronomy says, "The LORD will also bring on you every kind of sicknesses and disaster not recorded in this Book of the Law, until you are destroyed"/ Deuteronomy 28:61.

Envy

No one can really tell when God is angry. But anyone who does what is wrong can understand the state of God's mind as regards to that. This is true because most people have also become ignorant of certain odd lifestyles like envy which might be responsible for outbreak of deadly sicknesses.

'Envy!' do you know what that means? It means greed, jealousy or resentment: you love what others have with hate; you sneer, scoff, mock, disdain, ridicule, or laugh at them in disrespect, with a feeling that you're much better than others. By doing so you want you alone to be recognized and applauded. But how has envy become a root of sicknesses? Let's find out from these three siblings.

Moses had a long time been a great and successful leader. God chose him ahead of his elder brother and sister. Miriam and her brother, Aaron, were envious of their younger brother, Moses; because of the mighty way God used him to perform miraculous signs and wonders in the eyes of men. They said awful things against Moses, the man of God, and that provoked the anger of God on them. As a result God unleashed the sickness of leprosy on Miriam, and instantly she became a leprous/ Read: Numbers 12:1-15.

Most people have turned lunatic on streets, many got burnt in strange fire, and others buried alive for looking down or saying awful things against men of God/ Read: Numbers 16:1-35. Some, too, have been killed by wild animals because of similar reasons/ Read: 2nd Kings 2:23-24. Stop being envious!

It doesn't matter whether they are not your pastors or look big like other men of God. They may not appear like men of God per-se, but such act of envy is capable of incurring lasting pains. Envy makes people treat people with contempt and God hates that. Are you in the habit of this kind of life? Then you need healing.

Hatred

There is a slogan that says, "You can't eat your cake and have it." You may be asking a question why hatred may be a root of sicknesses. Let's be clear on this matter. Like envy, hatred is simply a thing of the mind. And when you hate someone, the state of your entire being will be decentralized because your mind controls you. At this point your whole being becomes unsettle and attracts any kind of sicknesses. [God is a God of love not hate]

In the story of the bible, Jacob loved Rachel very much but family tradition got him married to Leah. Because he was unsatisfied with Leah, he forged ahead and got married to Rachel, having two wives. The most annoying thing is Jacob concentrated his love to Rachel, and hated Leah, his first wife. God wasn't pleased with this kind of family settlement, so he caused the womb of Rachel to become barren, and instead opened the womb of the unloved wife to bear children/ Read: Genesis 29:26-31.

For twenty years Jacob's second wife suffered barrenness and was desperate to have children by all means. Though Jacob knew about this but could do nothing to help the situation. Somehow he began treating Leah with honour and at that, God answered the prayers of Rachel and remembered her/ Read: Genesis 30:1-2, 2-8, 20, 22-23.

So many barren cases today have a root linked to hatred, whereas this type of case is still a delusion to some medical scientists.

Stubbornness

Life is expected to be entirely flexible. And the people experiencing it must not live otherwise. If you are not open to receive and to take, then you're likely to be regarded as stubborn. Stubbornness means inflexibility, doggedness or arrogance. What do these further explain? It explains that a person who is stubborn is proud, and a proud person cannot switch to God philosophy or its resemblance. This character is often exhibited by tyrants and people of like minds.

On a second look; stubbornness can sometimes turn a good quality in the lives of adventurers. But not so with anyone who bluntly refuses to adhere to God's instruction. You can be rejected by God if you're stubborn. This is a fact/ Read: 1st Samuel 15:23.

King Saul is one perfect example. After he refused to carry out God's instruction, God sent him an evil spirit that tormented his life day and night until an anointed person plays a music from the harp/ Read: 1st Samuel 16:14-23.

During the 430 years in the land of Egypt. God told Pharaoh, the king of Egypt, to set free his slaves, who were the Jews. Pharaoh have never seen or heard of any other god but himself. This made him more obstinate to hearken to God's instruction.

When you make yourself stubborn to God's word, he makes you even more stubborn/ Read: Romans 1:28; Exodus 10:1. That's exactly what happened to Pharaoh. As a result of his stubbornness, God did outstanding miraculous signs and wonders in Egypt to prove him wrong. These miraculous signs and wonders unleashed deadly diseases to both men and animals. In spite of all that God did, Pharaoh refuses to change his mind/Read: Exodus 7-14; 9:7-35.

Stubborn people like these always end up losing everything. Do not let stubbornness to accepting God's word get hold of your life. You will definitely become God's enemy unknowing to you, and in the end, you will certainly bow to his command/ Read: Exodus 14:21-31.

Satan

According to the New International Version of the Holy Bible; the word 'Satan' is seen fourteen times in the Old Testament, and thirty two times in the New Testament. There could be much more or less mentioned in other versions or translations. Satan is a name given to a mighty cherub – the leader of the fallen angels first called Lucifer, the son of the morning. He lusted after the glory, fame, and supreme power of God and corrupted his precious wisdom because of pride/ Read: Isaiah 14:12-15; Ezekiel 28:12-17.

On the account of his plan leading protect to overthrow his maker, God. He, together with the other rebellious angels was thrown down forcefully to the earth. And from that time the human race have been a threat to his quest for power, fame, and glory. What was he really angry about? God took the world he planned to dominate and gave it to man to rule. At this Satan [the great dragon, the old serpent, the devil, and the deceiver of the brethren] became man's greatest rival till date/ Read: Revelation 12:7-9, 17.

He is a complete bunch of evil just as his name (Satan) implies. Satan doesn't think anything good of anyone. His plans are to steal from you, inflict you with sickness, get you to curse God, separate you from your true worship, and destroy you completely. Always very excited to see people get hurts. This is how the man called Job became his prey and got terribly sick. Satan was responsible for both the sores that came on his body and the disasters that claimed his entire household and business/ Read: Job 1:12-22; 2:5-7.

Satan is not a figure that can be recognized physically or facially; though he sometimes appears in various forms like a mighty dragon or serpent. The fact is he deals with millions of demons (evil spirits) to carry out his evil plans on the human race/ Read:

Mark 5:8-15. Each demon is a messenger representing a particular sin and responsible for a plague. Like the case of Job, one of these messengers was also sent to inflict the apostle Paul with a terrible thorn on his flesh/ Read: 2nd Corinthians 12:7.

You should know that Satan is a plague on people and does his evil biding against the righteous. This means he is the sole root or agent of every kind of sickness and troubles that comes to humans. Those serving Satan as their worship are already doomed because they're all enslaved.

Stealing

"Will a man rob God? Yet you rob me.' 'But you ask, 'How do we rob you?' 'In tithes and offerings. You are under a curse – the whole nation of you – because you are robbing me. Bring the whole tithe into the storehouse, that there may be food in my house. Test me in this,' says the LORD Almighty, 'and see if I will not throw open the floodgates of heaven and pour out so much blessing that you will not have room enough for it.'

"I will prevent pests from devouring your crops, and the vines in your fields will not cast their fruit,' says the LORD Almighty"/ Malachi 3:8-10.

God says you are robbing him in two ways: first, the 'Tithes', and second, the 'Offering'. The tithe is the One-tenth of your income or profit, which you are to bring to the Church or to a man of God. Both points of delivery are equally the storehouse. Understand this that tithes is God's portion in your income. Whenever you refuse to pay your tithes or pay less than a one-tenth as instructed, then you are placed under a curse.

The offering on the other hand is your general contributions to the work of God like sponsoring soul winning programs (evangelism), building mission houses, taking care of ministers of God as well as the needy. But I must warn you! If you must give – give cheerfully, not grudgingly, for God loves a cheerful giver. And remember to give where the offering is mostly needed/ Read: 2nd Corinthians 9:7. You do not give for people to see and praise you. Such type of giving is wrong and there is no blessing attached/ Read: Matthew 6:1-4.

God knows exactly your size of income. Why treat God like a dog? Now this is what I mean: you get fat income from your sources of investment and yet you decide to give a widow's might to the work of God and to the needy. Even the widow's might from widows are far bigger than your offerings. What a shame! This is a clear rubbery in offering that leads to losses in your family and businesses.

God will always refuse to prevent those pests that eat people's crops when it comes to your turn. At the same time you will plant [invest] but not harvest. These and many more are sicknesses inflicted on those who are bent on rubbing God.

You can't steal from God and get away with it. No matter how much profits you make, you will certainly loose them anyhow. God will definitely allow attacks from every side to be unleashed on you until you have spent ten times the money you stole from him. The bible says:

"Worship the LORD your God, and his blessing will be on your food and water. I will take away sickness from among you..."/ Exodus 23:25-26.

Chapter 2: REASONS YOU ARE SICK

There are questions people ask everyday and I think they really requires straight answers. Should a person ever fall sick? Or should the human body experience breakdown? Or is it possible for one to stay healthy always and live that way? I am pretty sure that you, too, may be asking the same questions. All the answers to these questions are with emphatically YES! Yes, you can fall sick. Yes, you can experience breakdown. And yes, you can stay healthy and live that way.

The other big question on this subject is what are the reasons you are sick? There are so many reasons why you are sick, but here are those most important reasons to note:

1. You are sick because you need to be purged

2. You are sick because you eat and drink excess

3. You are sick because you take part in the forbidden

4. You are sick because you eat Holy Communion into unclean body

5. You are sick because you're careless and unhygienic

6. You are sick because you don't fear God

7. You are sick because God must be glorified

You Are Sick Because You Need To Be Purged

You cannot pour a new wine into an old wine skin. The wine will lose its taste and they will both burst. Also, you cannot patch a new cloth with an old cloth. The cloth will tear quickly on all sides and its beauty will fade. These were the proverbs of Jesus Christ to the professors of religious law.

Don't think that God is the one using you just because you find yourself doing God's work successfully well after you jumped out of the bed committing fornication without any remorse or genuine repentance. Some people, in their ignorance, have thought it that way.

The truth is whenever God wants to use a person he first of all purges him. This means that your old life and its impurities need to be washed away completely before God can use. Purging is a way of cleansing the body or removing unwanted element from the body. The first cleansing method God requires here is fasting and prayer/ Read: Mark 2:18-22.

It takes an uneasy process to refine gold and silver in a furnace of fire. After gold has been refined, the final product is always attractive – glittering with a high market value. This is no different from the way God purges humans especially those he wants to use. God may not tell you he's breaking you down to refine you. No, he picks you up as a piece of silver or gold and throws you into his refining fire. It could be any kind of sickness you can never imagine/ Read Malachi 3:2-4.

Our bodies are like cars or motors used every day either for businesses or pleasures. But we often forget that even these engines needs to be serviced to serve us well. And a bad engine oil or fuel is capable of knocking down your car. However if you have a car and its engine is knocked, you will require a total run down of services, which the engine must be dropped. For a mechanic it means filtering, changing damaged parts, and replacing them with new ones. Sometimes the process takes longer than necessary to get the car back to life.

David, after realizing his sins, begged God to purge him. He knows that an impurity has entered inside him, and that, too, has stolen his joy of salvation. /
Read: Psalm 51:7-12.

May be I'm talking to someone who is physically sick on the body; or maybe I'm talking to someone who is spiritually sick right now. But, whether you're mentally or emotionally sick; God wants to purge you.

If that's what God is doing in your life right now, why not let him deal with you as he wishes. After all he won't kill you. God told Satan to go ahead and test Job with a sickness, but he must not touch his life/ Read Job 2:6-7. Job went through a terrible suffering from the sores inflicted on him, and in the end, God completed his refining process on him and restored back his life to a greater glory/ Read: Job 42:10-17. This is how God is going to heal you and restore you back if you are patient and let him purge you.

Elder James said, "Consider it pure joy, my brothers, whenever you face trials of many kinds, because you know that the testing of your faith develops perseverance. Perseverance must finish its works so that you may be mature and complete, not lacking anything"/ Read: 2nd Corinthians 4:8-9. Your affliction or sickness might be momentary or protracted. That doesn't really matter. What matters is it produces for you an eternal weight of glory beyond all imaginations/ Read: 2nd Corinthians 4:17.

You Are Sick Because You Eat And Drink Excess

Eating and drinking are pleasures and activities of everyday life. Eating is simply the act of taking or consuming solid edible substances into the body as part of giving strength or energy boost for work activities.

Drinking, on the other hand, is the taking of liquid substances like water, wine, or syrups – a kind of body refreshment that quenches thirst, complement pleasures, and quick digest food substances in the body/ Read: 1st Kings 19:8.

In biblical context, eating and drinking are the studying or partaking or living in an admirable lifestyle. It means doing something you love to do – something others may sometimes not approve of, making it offensive in most cases. Have you experienced this kind of eating and drinking lately?/ Read: Romans 14:15-21.

Let us concentrate on the activities of real or physical food and drink especially water. All living creatures depend on food and water for both growth and health. When you eat or drink water in line with what your body needs, then you are bound to live healthily. Excess eating and drinking gives the body great fatigue. You will notice it once you are unable to wriggle the body as usual.

There are many types of sicknesses that come with eating and drinking too much, and it's often impossible to escape from partaking. This actually happened to me.

I want to let you know that I have been praying for years, asking God to reduce the size of my tummy. My major problem was not just the potbelly; I was at the same time suffering from obesity (the sickness of portliness, heaviness, and fatness). I consume large quantity of food both at meal time and between meal times, and drink more than twenty liters of water a day. This is only good for cows but quite excessive on a human body!

But God did not answer the prayers until I decided to cut down my food size and water consumption by constant fasting and rigorous exercise of running. I ran 2000 meters daily for over six months and burnt out so many calories. And you, too, can embark on these exercises. They have a way of keeping you on food discipline and living you with good body shape. After all the Holy Scriptures says people do not live by food alone, but by every word that comes out of the mouth of the LORD/ Read: Deuteronomy 8:3.

When a medical doctor says drink much water because it's good for the body. It doesn't mean you should gobble up water as cows do. Dr. Paul of Tarsus, gave his godson, Timothy, a medical prescription for his sick condition. He said, "Stop drinking only water, and use a little wine because of your stomach and your frequent illness"/ 1st Timothy 5:23.

Talking about taking little wine; most people have misinterpreted and misuse this portion of the bible. Biblically wine stands for both sweet drinks and alcohol. In many occasions these have been used interchangeably. It is true that by medical research the content in alcohol drinks can stabilize and heal bad health condition. This has to do with a little quantity of the smallest tea-cup content of about 100 to 150 milligrams, may be twice a week, as Dr. Paul prescribed for Timothy.

But people who take wine or alcoholic drinks for pleasures are exposing themselves to harm. This is because the sweetness of such drinks controls their thirst and drives them to drink excess, which gives birth to drunkenness, hallucination, misbehaviors, debauchery, vomiting, mental disorder, diabetes, and many other sicknesses like these. If you are not driven crazy by the sweetness of what you eat or drink, then you are liable to be free from the punishment that follows/ Read: Proverbs 23:19-21, 29-35; 25:16; Job 20:14-15;

God wants you to be filled with the Holy Spirit so your life will be guided positively, rather than giving into the influence of strong drinks, which misguides and leads your life to the opposite direction. I have heard people say they can drink as many bottles of bear as possible and still not drunk. How possible that is? Everything you do, eat or drink in excess has a way of intoxicating your life. That is sickness.

The bible says, "And be not drunk with wine, wherein is excess; but be filled with the Spirit"/ Ephesians 5:18.

Take time to study and understand how your body responds or reacts to the size of food you eat and the quantity of your drinks. Don't eat more than what your body can take; and don't drink more than what your brain and entire body can absorb. This is recommendable!

But you can control your thirst for drinking excess by developing a habit of drinking at least 750 milligrams (0.75liters) of water first thing every morning. It cleanses the body cistern. Try as much as possible to avoid eating and drinking cold water or cola drinks like mineral at the same time. It doesn't allow food digest easily. Drink warm water instead while eating. Or drink it before breakfast every morning. It's the nature's most powerful remedy.

Take a look at the six things drinking warm water can do for your body on the table. These six water therapy prescriptions are a summary of Stella Metsovas, a clinical nutritionist and media health expert in food and nutrition sciences, media health publication.

CLEANSES DIGESTION	Breaks down food faster and make digestion easy
AIDS CONSTIPATION	Improve bowel movements and returns your body back to normal functioning
ALEVIATES PAINS	From menstruation to headaches, calming and soothing effect on the abdominal muscles, and provide instant relief

	from cramps and muscles spasms.
SHED EXCESS POUNDS	Increases both body temperature and metabolism rate
IMPROVES BLOOD CIRCULATION	Flushes out toxins and enhance blood circulation
HALTS PREMATURE AGING	Repair skin cells and increase elasticity

You Are Sick Because You Take Part In The Forbidden

What is forbidden? It's something illegal, prohibited, not allowed or permitted to take part or consume.

There are so many things that are not permissible for your consumption. They may be good for your friend, but not good for you. And whenever you eat or take those things which are not permitted for your use, you will definitely get sick. This is what God says:

"And the LORD commanded the man, 'You are free to eat from any tree in the garden; but you must not eat the fruit from the tree of the knowledge of good and evil, for when you eat of it you will surely die'"/ Genesis 2:16-17.

For instance the medical institutions have put up a public

announcement that smoking is dangerous to health, and secondly that smokers are liable to die young.

In spite of this widespread information many smokers have continued to smoke increasingly. I have heard cigarette smokers saying that smoking makes them high and feel better. The question here is; are the medical doctors telling lies about smoking? And if their discovery is far from truth as some have claimed; will God also tell lies by keeping you from smoking or eating the forbidden? Think about it!

The bible also has something quite interesting in another

perspective. Everything might be permissible for your participation, but for the health and safety of your own body, it is better to refrain from eating them. Would you say that your body was made for food or for sexual immorality? Of course not! Your body was meant for the Lord and the Lord for your body/
Read: 1st Corinthians 6:12-13, 15-16.

So if others are simply doing those things that God forbids, does this give you a license to do them as well?

Stop looking at the type of food others eat. Not all foods are good for you. There are specific kinds of foods that works well in your body, and you need to discover them. Desist from eating foods that doesn't add to your body.

By the original plan of God, every one of us was created to eat fruits. I believe the right kinds of food suitable for man's healthy body are the vegetables and fresh fruits, which contain important vitamins, minerals and plant chemicals, as well as fiber. These include vitamin A (beta-carotene), C and E, magnesium, zinc, phosphorus and folic acid. Folic acid may reduce blood levels of homocysteine, a substance that may be a risk factor for coronary heart disease.

A diet high in vegetables can help protect you against cancer, diabetes and heart disease. It is advisable to eat five kinds of vegetables and two kinds of fruits everyday for good health. Fruits and vegetables should be an important part of your daily diet. When buying and serving fruits and vegetables; aim for variety to get the most nutrients and appeal. Note: some ripe or yellow fruits like pineapple and banana have highly concentrated sugars. If you are diabetic, eat less ripe or yellow fruits, but eat more green fruits.

Yellow, red and green fruits or vegetables have antioxidants which help in fighting free radicals in the body. Not only that. These fruits and vegetables eaten over the years will protect your immune cistern and/or system from collapsing easily. When you maintain eating foods like these, you save more money from buying drugs.

It is very important to note that fruits and vegetables have all the types of medicine our bodies need to keep up a healthy living on daily bases.

In line with eating right for your healthy living, you also need to eat according to your blood type. Most researches have not really confirmed this. But Doctor Peter J. D'Adamo's "Eat Right 4 Your Type" have proven to be very useful. I have tried my 'B Positive' food list and it's very amazing.

We have most of these fruits and vegetables still available. And if you had no slightest idea of any of them, I have written out a few in their categories on the table, from the Australian dietary guidelines, 2013, National Health and Medical Research Council, and Lock K. Pomerleau J, Causer L, et al, 2005 – a bulletin of W.H.O,, vol 83.

FRUITS	VEGETABLES
APPLES AND PEARS	LEAFLY GREEN: Lettuce, spinach and silverbeet
CITRUS FRUITS: Oranges, grapefruits, mandarins	CRUCIFEROUS: Cabbage, cauliflower, Brussels sprouts and broccoli

and limes	
STONE FRUITS: Nectarines, apricots, peaches and plums	**MARROW:** Pumpkin, cucumber and zucchini
TROPICAL EXOTIC: Bananas and mangoes	**ROOT:** Potato, sweet potato and yam
BERRIES: Strawberries, raspberries, blueberries, kiwifruit and passion fruit	**EDIBLE PLANT STEM:** Celery and asparagus
MELONS: Watermelons, rockmelons and honeydew melons	**ALLIUM:** Onion, garlic and shallot
TOMATOES AND AVOCADOS:	

The table of fruits and vegetables you just read are a breakdown of food discoveries God commanded humans to eat.

Some of them like LEGUMES: fresh beans and peas, soy products, flours, dried beans and peas, are required to be cooked before eating, though you can still eat a raw fresh vegetable leaf. Following God's plan and instruction in foods will keep you from falling sick.

After God has finished creating everything, he said to man: "...I give you every seed-bearing plant on the face of the whole earth and every tree that has fruit with seed in it. they will be yours for food.'"/ Genesis 1:29. You see, God knows exactly what is good for your consumption. This why you must be careful with the kind of foods you eat.

The Garden of Eden where God placed Adam and Eve didn't have hamburgers, ice creams, do-nuts, cakes, hotdogs, meat-pies, stews with spices, or thousands of foods we prefer to eat today. Every food God recommended for man to eat was simply the best.

"And the LORD God commanded the man, "You are free to eat from any tree [any fruits bearing plant] in the Garden."/ Genesis 2:18

Daniel and his three friends were given opportunity to eat the richest kind of food from the king's palace. Anyone who eats the king's food and drinks his wine for at least six months is expected to have smooth skin and plump. On the contrary these four young men rejected the king's food, and instead, requested for only vegetable and water. Within ten days, feeding on only vegetable and water, their looks was much better than those who have been on the king's meal for months/ Read: Daniel 1:8-16; Zachariah 9:7.

But what would happen if they have eaten the king's rich foods? They would defile their bodies and get spiritually sick because the king's foods and drinks were at the same time dedicated to his gods. Once you become conscious of such kind of food, don't eat it for conscience sake else you'll get sick/ Read: 1ˢᵗ Corinthians 10:28-29. After all it's not what goes into your body that really defiles you, but what comes out of your body.

However, you must understand that some foods that looks very enticing and delicious can turn sour in your stomach if you refused to put a knife on your throat/ Read: Matthew 15:10-11, 17-20.

There is another way out; you can eat whatever is presented to you without asking questions whether the foods or drinks have been offered to idols/ Read: 1ˢᵗ Corinthians 10:25, 27; 8:7-10. Know this; too, that every food we eat is pure unless you're feeling different.

And, if you always feel different, you can't really trust God's gift/ Read: Romans 14:14. But if your conscience insist and is unstable in this kind of situation, you should pray. Yes, pray on every food or drink presented to you. Everything is made pure through the word and prayers/ Read: 1st Timothy 4:4-5; Titus 1:15

There is safety in praying on whatever you receive or buy from the market. They may be food, drink, wears, and anything meant for your use or consumption. First, receive them with thanksgiving. Second, ask God to bless them for your nourishment. Third, ask for supply for those who do not have. If you pray like this with your mind; your prayer has great power to neutralize poisons or viruses.

You Are Sick Because You Eat Holy Communion Into Unclean Body

A Holy Communion is the Lord's Supper taken by every Christian as a symbol of remembering the death of Jesus Christ. It is made up of bread as the body of Christ, and wine as the blood of Christ. The Holy Communion is a very powerful food and drink combination that is capable of healing, and at the same time strike unholy people with sicknesses. One of the qualifications of partaking in the Lord's Table requires the

Christian partaker to prepare spiritually or be spiritually purged before taking part.

It's a great and powerful Christian ritual. Before you partake, you are expected to forgive anyone you have hurt, clean up your mind as well as your heart, and ask God for forgiveness, mercy, and total cleansings from all your wrongs. And if you go ahead to take the Holy Communion when you're not sanctified, you will be exposed to the attack of any sickness. Here's what the bible says:

"Therefore, whoever eats the bread or drinks the cup of the Lord in an unworthy manner will be guilty of sinning against the body and the blood of the Lord. A man ought to examine himself before he eats of the bread and drinks of the cup.

"For anyone who eats and drinks without recognizing the body of the Lord eats and drinks judgment on himself. That is why many of you are weak and sick, and a number of you have fallen asleep"/ 1ˢᵗ Corinthians 11:26-30.

I have seen and heard how the power of Holy Communion struck down people who took it unworthily. But I am not creating any fear in you.

The word of God testifies strongly about this. Many

Christians are even ignorant. In spite of what you already know, the Holy Communion also serves as a healing food and blood tonic supplement.

Through participating in the Lord's Supper, you can be sure to have a rich life in Christ Jesus, both in this life and in the life after.

Grab this lesson today. Do not partake in the Holy Communion until you're prepared and cleansed! Note: A communion supplement, element, sacrament or Eucharist that is not powerful, is the one prepared and consecrated by an unholy priest. Such elements or 'holy foods' as they are called have no negative or positive effects on people who take them.

You Are Sick Because You Are Careless And Unhygienic

To be careless is to be hasty and not being careful. Carelessness has caused a lot of people injuries. Many have been infected with viruses and different type of sicknesses as a result of not being careful. It leads to many regrets, and you, too, might have been stabbed by your careless lifestyle. Carelessness goes with doing something and not thinking of the safety rules that might implicate or destroy in the outcome/ Read: Proverbs 19:3.

Unhygienic means you're living an unhealthy or unclean lifestyle. Do you know that God also requires cleanliness as scorecard for your healthy living and spiritual victories? Careless and unhygienic lifestyles travel on one route.

For instance a person using modern facilities like toilets with water closet will be expected to flush the toilet properly after usage, wash it regularly with best treated chemicals, and stay free from germs contamination. This is in line with the instructions God has given/ Read: Deuteronomy 28:12-14. If God is protecting you from falling sick, do not take that for granted. You need to protect yourself as well.

There are so many men infected with the skin sickness called bums. This sickness is usually on the back side of the head and the bearded side from the cheek to the chin.

People who do shaving quite often are likely to have burns. It can also be contracted from an infected person to the hair barber's clipper. Once the clipper is used on you, you are likely to be infected from the cut or shaved point. There it usually begins to grow and itches. Dare to scratch it, it grows big and bubbles like balloons.

You need a Spiritual immunization, and that's the

best kind of protection you can depend upon. It doesn't matter if some of the sicknesses are airborne. You can contract any kind of disease once you are careless and unhygienic.

The bible says, "Whoever digs a pit may fall into it; whoever breaks through a wall may be bitten by a snake. Whoever quarries stones may be injured by them; whoever splits logs may be endangered by them"/ Ecclesiastes 10:8-9.

You Are Sick Because You Don't Fear God

The word 'fear' can be regarded as the act of accepting to come under an awful influence. It can be taken as a high regard placed on a frightening unseen being.

Fear simply means to become afraid of something or somebody with an intention of placing your loyalty in worship.

We do not fear men; we respect men, and fear God instead. The bible says to fear the LORD is to hate evil/ Read: Proverbs 8:13. There is a clear difference between respect and fear. When you fear someone, you will hate to offend him. But you can show respect to people and still offend them behind their backs. If you hate evil just like God does, why should you get sick or be open to attack of sickness? It's absolutely impossible except by God's own permission/ Read: Psalm 91:1-10.

God loved Job so much because he has always been careful to live a life without sin. As a result Job had the highest immunity from God, which shielded him from the attack of Satan.

It all started like a drama when Satan took a complaint to God about Job, saying, "Does Job fear God for nothing?' Satan replied. 'Have you not put a hedge [a strong wall, protection] around him and his household and everything he has? You have blessed the work of his hands, so that his flocks and herds are spread throughout the land"/ Read: Job 1:9-10.

Everyone that fears God and hate to do evil is like Job in this world. You cannot experience the bad attacks others are experiencing unless it's permitted by God. Ask God about the attack that befalls you whenever you refuse to compromise with evil. If you are truly holy and still have sicknesses or any attack from the enemy, then you don't have to worry about it. It means God has a hand in your troubles, and he'll surely give you quick restoration.

Real protection is secured for all those who truly fear God. If you are not afraid of God and continue in the practicing of evil, you are just like a building without walls or fence/ Read: 1ˢᵗ John 5:18.

You need to know God. And the best way to know him is to practice his written words. It may seem difficult as some people claim. All you need is patience. Yes, it takes patience to know God.

You Are Sick Because God Must Be Glorified

A certain blind man had an encounter with Jesus Christ. His followers questioned the man's blindness and wanted to know if he or his parents have sinned, since he was born that way. Jesus answered and told them that none of them sinned. Rather his blindness was waiting for the fulfillment of God's glory. This means that the cause of his blindness was not as a result of his sins or his parents/ Read: John 9:1-3.

There are car services you won't require from a second-hand mechanic. You will need the professional touch of the manufacturer. A manufacturer makes his name when his products are used, and also when the product requires a delicate services attention. Ask yourself this question: "Is my sickness or affliction waiting for the fulfillment of God's glory?" And if your sickness does not bring God his deserved glory, who else will it glorify?

Hold on a second... is it not better to suffer for a little time, a sickness that is hopeful that in the end, healing is sure to come from God?

Everything in life happens for a reason. I believe this is the opportunity you've been waiting for. Wherever you are right now; God must be glorified in your life. That's why he created you – isn't it? So let him glorify himself. Soon his divine healing in your life will reveal his glory.

This is how Jesus Christ healed the blind man who had waited in pains for God's glory to be seen. He spit on the ground, and made some mud with the saliva, and put on the man's eyes, and told him to wash in the pool of Siloam. And as the man went and wash his eyes, he began to see clearly. Everyone who saw him was amazed at the healing and began to praise God. Others questioned his healing because they knew it was impossible for a man born blind to see.

But the blind man, having believed in the one God used, who is Jesus Christ, the Son of God, fell and worshiped at his feet/ Read: John 9:6-41.

God's power and miraculous healing is always the best solution to rely on. When you have applied every form of medical prescription and your sickness refuses to leave, just know that the doctor of doctors needs to come in. And you must fall back to God's miraculous healing even if it will need to take some time, so that God will be glorified as the LORD who heals you.

Chapter 3: THE BRUISER AND THE HEALER

In this chapter the bruiser and the healer, you are going to learn about a slogan that says *the one who bites is the one who heals.* But how can this possibly be? From what we already know, the bruiser (that is the person who injures or wounds, or make sick) is always different from the healer (that is the person who treats, make well, or cures).

And why would someone deliberately injures you, and at the same time wants to heal your wounds? This doesn't sound good to you, right?

You must have seen it happen several times. It is not always the person who knocks you down by car that treats you. What I mean is a medical doctor might crash on you with his car, but he may not be the one to give you back your life. Secondly, a person who deliberately shoots you with a gun will not want you get healed.

In a story of the bible, the Good Samaritan picked up a man by the road side, which was beaten and badly wounded by armed robbers.

He took him to a nearby healing home and had his wounds

stitched, well dressed, and treated. After doing all that he paid some amount of money for the treatments and promised to pay for additional expenses that might arise in the course of making him well.

Don't forget this; the thieves bruised the man, but another man (the Good Samaritan), became the healer/ Read: Luke 10:30-35.

We often find it on a very rare case where someone, after deliberately brutalizing your face, takes you to the hospital. This happens in marriages between couples. Some couples call it real love. And if this is actually real love for married couples, that after bruising each other, they're still in love, living together as man and wife; it also proves that where love is at work, one can be bruised with the intentions of keeping alive.

The bible says, "See now that I myself am He! There is no god besides me. I put to death and I bring to life, I have wounded and I will heal, and no one can deliver out of my hand"/ Deuteronomy 32:39.

God is the bruiser and the healer. He is a killer and life giver. But does God bruise you intentionally because he's wicked? And does he also kill you intentionally because he hates you? A good father beats his child with a rod when the child is rude or goes wrong. If the beatings is deepened and wounds are sustained; he makes sure the child is properly treated with correction.

You have a heavenly Father who is more fatherly than your earthly father, and he is God.

Now, at least you can understand how God's love is strong on you. Just as you see the sun and moon dim, and after a while they brighten up again. Even if God bruises you, there is hope that he'll surely heal you; and even if he kills you, he'll surely bring you back to life/ Read: Isaiah 30:26. So it is better to get bruises from God.

The truth is before God bruises you, he makes the cure available.

God's way of bruising is like a fatherly discipline that brings about correction. And does he just go ahead and bruises you for nothing? Of course, not!

God does that to correct you whenever you go wrong; and with the scars left after the bruises, he knows you will always retrace your steps from evil/ Read: Hebrews 12:5-8.

A Direct Punch

Bruises are in various forms and it doesn't really matter how they come on you. God can decide to give you a direct punch. The punches from God are sometimes heavier or lighter depending on the wrongs.

But in the case of Jesus Christ, it was a heavy punch from God. His bruises were not because he did anything wrong! You want to know why would God do such a thing to his only begotten Son?

Okay. Here is the answer: God is always choosing a way or formula that is not familiar to men, to deal with things that are higher than the imaginations of men, and to the glorification of his name.

What man will descend heavily with deep bruises on his only child in the name of practical experiment or as formula to solve problems for the same people who want his son dead? This is incredulous, huh?

You, me, and your entire family members are one of the reasons God took such a decision on his dear Son, Jesus Christ. All he wants is that through the bruises of his Son, you might get healing at anytime; and also that after the bruises; you might be reconciled to him at anytime. These bruises on Jesus are the punishment God would have given to you, but he chooses to let him bear the pains for your sake.

What if I tell you that Jesus Christ was also suffering from some sought of sickness within him and no one knew about it? From the mouth of the prophet Isaiah, who spoke of his suffering a long time ago I have come to understand this mystery.

Chapter 53:4 clearly wrote: "Surely he took up our infirmities [sicknesses, illnesses, medical condition, diseases, etc.] and carried our sorrows [mornings, sadness, troubles, pains, grieves, disappointments, etc.], yet we considered him stricken by God, smitten by him, and afflicted.

It is quite clear that Jesus Christ was carrying about sicknesses within him because of man. Sicknesses God deliberately removed from us and put on him to bear for us all.

I have heard some pastors and Christians say one who is in Christ can never be sick. This is complete ignorance of the scripture. A man can become sick by simply following the footsteps of Jesus Christ or by bearing other people's pains.

The bible says, "We always carry around in our body the death of Jesus, so that the life of Jesus may also be revealed in our body."/ 2nd Corinthians 4:10. If you get sick anyhow, just praise God that you have been permitted to share in the sufferings of Jesus Christ.

Usually a person needs to be charged with wrong before he's tortured. But this case is completely different. Not that he sinned against God. God made him guilty by putting your sins on him, so that through his sufferings you, too, might find salvation, which is your spiritual healing, as well as the healing to your sick body. By this reason, Jesus received a direct punch from God. And he humbly and patiently went through the pains/ Read: Isaiah 53:3-12; 2nd Corinthians 4:8-11; 1st Peter 2:21-25.

The Direct Punch

Have you ever been beaten or wounded for being innocent of a crime leveled against you? This crime against humanity happens almost every day. Innocent people get hurt by hate brutalization. Their bruisers are always happy to see it happen. And in many case, people who punches you without a cause often feels they're doing God a service/ Read: John 16:2.

The bible encouragement to such godless crime says, "But even if you should suffer for what is right, you are blessed. 'Do not fear what they fear; do not be frightened. It is better, if it is God's will, to suffer for doing good than for doing evil"/ 1st Peter 3:14, 17. In support to this, the Law also says that anyone who hit someone and wounds him will need to pay and see to it that he is completely healed/ Read: Exodus 21:18-19.

If I may ask, are you one of those bruising others without a cause? Since you need healing from God; you don't need to do that anymore. You can be the one to heal those people already bruised by you.

In summary, this is a very important point to note: God will bruise people according to the weight of their wrongs. This means heavy bruises will be given to you for your heavy sins/ Read: Mark 12:40. On the other hand, light bruises will be given to you for your light sins/ Read: Luke 23:22. Come to think of it; does your bruise actually match with the weight of your sins? Or is God just being merciful?/ Read: Luke 23:41; 2nd Corinthians 2:5-6; Hebrews 10:29.

Chapter 4: LOOK AT THE BRAZEN SERPENT

In the previous chapter you read about the bruiser and the healer; saying that the one who bites is the one who heals! And this is true. Nevertheless there is something different to learn in this chapter. Now you need to look steadily at the one who bites to bring about the healing you're dying to receive.

First, let's take a look at what happened. As usual, whenever the people rebel against the LORD, he bites them and uses his venom to cure their wounds.

Here's what the bible says, "So the LORD sent poisonous snakes among the people, and many were bitten and died. Then the people came to Moses and cried out, 'We have sinned by speaking against the LORD and against you. Pray that the LORD will take away the snakes.' So Moses prayed for the people/ Read: Numbers 21:6-7-NLT.

Note the line of the bible portion in the previous paragraph saying: "...The LORD sent poisonous snakes among the people, and many were bitten and died." This is a clear confirmation that God ordered those snakes to strike the people down. At least you can believe now that God can strike you from any angle.

Don't be afraid; I'm not trying to make you scared, although you should be.

God needs a total repentance from your rebellion. As soon as you do this your healing will begin. This brings us to the next line of the bible portion saying, "Then the people came to Moses and cried out, 'We have sinned by speaking against the LORD and against you. Pray that the LORD will take away the snakes.' So Moses prayed for the people.'"

Prayer works a big deal. But an advocate of such magnitude like Moses is highly needed to avert the anger of God. God was also looking for a substitute – someone or something to look upon for their healing, and the solution came:

"Then the LORD told him, 'Make a replica of a poisonous snake and attach it to a pole. All who are bitten will live if they simply look at it!' So Moses made a snake out of bronze and attached it to a pole. Then anyone who was bitten by a snake could look at the bronze snake and be healed!'"/ Numbers 21:8-9-NLT.

Look at the brazing serpent! That's exactly what you are asked to do. A bronze is an alloy of two metals; a reddish-brown alloy essentially of copper and tin. Sometimes a bronze is made with a similar alloy of copper and other metals like aluminum or magnesium. It is often used as a figure, sculpture, head, or an icon/ *The New International Webster's Encyclopedia Dictionary of The English Language, pp.170.*

What does this imply to a brazing serpent? The main reason God told Moses to make a replica of the snake is simply telling the people that the one who bites is the one who heals. A copper might be fused with tin or aluminum or magnesium. Since there are two metals in one; each does a separate work. One might have a negative part, while the other gives a positive result. The picture is very clear. The one who bites you is God, and the one who heals you is God. This simply means the one you should look upon for your healing is God (The Brazing Serpent).

The Cure is Like A Computer Antivirus

First Aid Treatment (FAT) has taught us that it is always a hard and risky attempt to take off the viper's venom from the person bitten by it. The cure you are told to look at is like a computer antivirus. You need an antivirus to protect both your computer and documents.

Whenever a computer system has contacted a virus, the engineer or computer owner will need to look out for help from the antivirus company to heal the system.

The first step is usually to backup your files and format the system. The second step requires you install the antivirus into your computer so that it can scan and heal all infected files. Right now you are just like the computer system that needs antivirus to flush out every infection injected by the viper's venom causing malfunctioning in your entire cistern.

God wants you to look at the brazing serpent as your antivirus. Looking at the brazing serpent is looking at the cure – the exact figure where the bite came. In God's own theory, it is yet an unravel philosophy to prove that the same poisonous venom that infect you can as well be used to cure you. This book may have painted the brazing serpent or the cure as antivirus, but the intent of the healing source you are told to look at is far beyond the comparison of a computer antivirus.

Don't Make Yourself A Brazing Serpent

I never said you should go making yourself a brazing serpent and hang it on a pole. That's not the point. God has already made a provision as a replica of the brazing serpent which you can look upon today and be healed. You want to know him? He is Jesus Christ, the Son of God. The bible says this about him: "Just as Moses lifted up the snake in the desert, so the Son of Man must be lifted up, that everyone who believes in him may have eternal life..."/ John 3:14-18-NLT.

The Son of Man has often been used to describe the person of Jesus Christ in the bible. And he is the sacrificial lamb who was crucified between two criminals on the cross (tree), on a Good Friday. Moses lifted up the brazing serpent in the desert – a replica of the snake that strikes the people. That simple act represented Christ being lifted up on the tree.

In the same way, anyone who looked at the brazing serpent and lived, such will also live, when he looks at the crucified Lord, Jesus Christ. By this revelation we see that the true picture of the brazing serpent is actually Jesus Christ.

So, dear friend, what does it take to look at the one who bites you? It absolutely takes nothing. Looking here means depending on him for your healing, telling him how sorry you are, believing in him for your salvation, clinging on him for the recovery of every area of your life, and holding tight to his words for eternal life. Those are exactly what it takes and at the same time what you need to do.

Do not just look at the brazing serpent because you want healing

right away. You should keep looking steadily until he's finished dealing with you and fulfill all that you truly deserve. It is useless to charm a snake after striking you. A snake charming is very useful when the snake had not yet bitten anyone/
Read: Ecclesiastes 10:11.

Chapter 5: HERE COMES YOUR HEALING

There is a river of healing flowing with great power. Everyone who enters into this river of healing will never come out the same. First, I want to bring you into the river of healing. This river of healing is Jesus Christ, and you need to have faith in God. Do you believe you can be healed from that sickness tormenting your life? If your answer is yes, then your healing has just begun!

Secondly as you read this book, you will be directed by the Spirit to take certain steps to actualize your healing. Don't argue with whatever direction you're given. God's ways are not the ways of man. It may not really make sense – what you'll be asked to do. But if it's really the Spirit of God leading you, just walk in faith and divine healing will come.

Divine healing comes from the spiritual – it's a spiritual cure – a type of healing that amazes medical scientists whenever medical prescriptions becomes null and void and a victim of sickness or disease is miraculously restored.

Get Into The River of Healing

Centuries ago a certain military high commander of the army of the king of Aram, Naaman, suffered from the sickness of leprosy, and needed to be cured by all means. Imagine a top army officer of that rank, who must have had the opportunities to travel abroad, country by country for medical treatment, and yet, no one was able to cure him of his leprosy.

One day he was told by his slave girl to visit a prophet of God named Elisha. But he looked down on the advice probably because of his high level office, and went instead to see the king of Israel, whose meeting didn't go on well. When the prophet Elisha heard that the king of Israel was angry at the visit of Naaman seeking for medical treatment, he sent this massage to the king:

"Why have you torn your robes? Have the man come to me and he will know that there is a prophet in Israel.' So Naaman went with his horses and chariots and stopped at the door of Elisha's house. Elisha sent a messenger to say to him, 'Go, wash yourself seven times in the Jordan, and your flesh will be restored and you will be cleansed'"/ 2nd kings 5:1-10.

What the heck! This is disrespect to a high military officer. You're telling a country's number one commander like me to go and wash in the so called dirty river of Jordan. And by the way I thought you would just wave your hands at me and called on the name of your God and heal me right away. No, I can't do it. Why can't I go bath in the other clean and fine rivers or probably my swimming pool?'

You're reading about the pride of some people, how they cause hindrances to their blessings. Now if only you can humble yourself and do what the Spirit of God is asking you to do, your healing will come right away. Naaman got angry and left. But his servants begged him to obey the instruction from the Man of God.

After series of persuasions, Naaman got into the river of

Jordan, dipped himself seven times, as the man of God instructed, and he was healed of his leprosy; his flesh became clean like that of a young boy. Naaman said, "Now I know that there is no God in all the world except in Israel..."/ Read: 2nd kings 5:11-15.

Water has a great power to cleans, make well, and refresh. You can meet a Man of God and ask him to sanctify the water you want to use and it will act as your healing cleanser. Naaman dipped himself seven times into the river as instructed and he was cleansed. You can do the same by faith. Get into the river of healing now and wash yourself seven times. Dive seven times if you like, or get seven buckets of water and wash seven times.

Whether the river or water is dirty or clean; God will surely heal you. And be sure that your faith is in him alone. But I also want to remind you that God does not work in one way to heal you. So if you have been used to bathing hot water, try bathing normal water. If you have been bathing once or twice a day, try bathing as many times as possible. And if your faith says 'Seven times!' just go ahead.

Remember that this is faith healing. Do this and your healing will take place gradually and even instantly. One of the miracles of healing that will happen to your body is your sickness will disappear and your skin will be renewed like that of a baby. You can have the same water and use it for drinking. As you drink, it will wash away internal sicknesses in your body. There is no prescription or dosage, just drink it by faith.

Usually when angels come to trouble the water, people will carry their sick into the water so they can be healed. This was used to happening at the Pool of Bethsaida, until the coming of Jesus Christ.

Today I speak to the water you're about to bath to begin to trouble. Get into the river of healing right now and receive your healing.

And if there's no water around you there, just have faith; believe it that Jesus Christ is right there to lift you up from that sickness.

Do you really want to get well? The hand of God is resting on your body now. God is moving from ward to ward, and don't let him pass you by. Something is about to happen! I pray for you now. Receive your healing in Jesus Christ name/ Read: John 5:1-9.

Get Healed By The Balm

A balm is usually a combination of selected healing portions in form of cream or gel which, when applied on the sick spot, it gives relieve to the sick patient. There are so many sicknesses that require the application of a healing balm. And this is one of God's ways of demonstrating his healing power. If a prophet of God tells you to prepare a local balm and spread on your sick spot, go ahead and do it.

King Hezekiah was very, very sick, and had boils like skin cancer all over his body. God sent the prophet Isaiah to tell him that his sickness will lead to death, and that he won't recover from it. Hezekiah turned to God in prayers of weeping with many petitions.

When God saw how Hezekiah had prayed he changed his mind

and sent Isaiah back to him with a promise of living another fifteen years.

"Then Isaiah said, 'Make an ointment [balm] from figs,' so Hezekiah's servants spread the ointment [balm] over the boil, and Hezekiah recovered"/ 2nd kings 20:7. Note that before there was a sickness, there was also a healing. God cures your diseases even before you're treated. The balm application is a physical way of demonstrating God's healing power by fixing back your health to normal condition.

If God says you're healed, then you're healed. In such a case, it doesn't matter how severe the sickness is at that moment. Once an ointment is applied to the sick body, the word of God is activated. There are so many balms in the world. Some have been made to suit your wounds or type of sickness.

There is another biblical case of a man who was born blind, as I said previously, and who had been healed by the special balm. The bible says, "Having said this, he spit on the ground, made some mud with saliva, and put it on the man's eyes. 'Go', he told him, 'wash in the Pool of Siloam.' [This word means sent] So the man went and washed, and came home seeing'"/ John 9:6-11.

It's surprising when you hear that a blind man's eye was

opened by an application of a mere mixture of saliva and mud. But this time the instruction didn't end by just applying the mud.

Jesus, after mixing his saliva with mud and applying it on the man's eyes said to him, "Go, wash in the Pool of Siloam.'" This type of healing instruction is a little bit unusual. It's a combination of both the balm and wash.

God wants to heal you by the balm. Go ahead and use the balm prescribed for you by your medical doctor or a true prophet of God. Follow instructions carefully and there comes your healing.

Read A Doze of Scriptures And Get Healed

You can also get healed by reading God's word. Don't just open the bible and read, instead read, study, and meditate upon any scripture that flips your sight.

"My son, pay attention to what I say; listen closely to my words. Do not let them out of your sight, keep them within your heart; for they are life to those who find them and health to a man's whole body"/ Proverbs 4:20-22.

There is a strong force behind every letter of the bible. It gets activated and burns like liquid fire, and destructive like a mighty sledge hammer, as you read them and connect them with your mind. Like liquid fire, it purifies your whole body, spirit, and soul; and afterwards, like a mighty sledge hammer, it smashes into pieces every stone that wages war in your heart against God/ Read: Jeremiah 23:29.

Reading God's written word has a great advantage on your health condition. It practically deals with every type of health situations like hypertension, emotional trauma, heart break, night mares, and depression, which you hardly find medicines to cure. The bible says "For the word of God is living and active. Sharper than any double-edge sword, it penetrate even to dividing soul and spirit, joints and marrow; it judges the thoughts and attitudes of the heart"/ Hebrew 4:12.

If you say you have no sin, you make God a lair. Only by reading, studying, and meditating upon the Scriptures will your conscience become clear. You will know the truth and the secrets of God, and the truth will set you free/ Read John 8:32-36.

Touch The Fringe of His Garment

A certain woman suffered demurrage (a sickness of the issue of blood – a constant menstruation or bleeding) for twelve years. She has been to so many doctors, spending her last fortune for treatment but the situation never got any better. When she heard about the man called Jesus Christ, she followed after him in the tumult crowd and said to herself: "If I just touch his cloth, I will be healed."

So with a struggle, she stretches forth her hands to touch the fringe of his Garment. Acting upon such a great faith, she became healed, instantly.

Because of this great faith, Jesus Christ immediately experienced a drawn out healing power from him; he noticed that someone in the crowd had just tapped a high voltage healing current from his clothes/ Read: Mark 5:25-34.

Confusion erupts in the crowd as Jesus stopped and asked, "Someone has just touched me." Imagine you almost swallowed up by a great crowd and then turning to ask the same question. It will sound ridiculous to those around you. The truth is it will be highly or almost impossible to be surrounded by crowd who will never be able or have access to touch you or your clothes.

There were so many followers of Jesus Christ in the crowd with sicknesses and diseases just as we have today in churches and crusade grounds. Almost those very close to him have touched his garment over and over and yet nothing happened. But this woman touched his garment and became healed. Her thought of touching Jesus' garment was the faith that brought her healing.

Every Man of God possesses a great power whenever the anointing is at work. There are special cases like that of Jesus Christ where even the clothes, handkerchiefs, aprons, chairs, beds, and everything the Man of God touches or uses, flows with a healing anointing.

Whoever believes and touches any of these things will be healed; just the same way the woman with the issue of blood got healed/
Read: Matthew 14:35-36.

The apostle Paul is one good example. God gave him power to do unusual miracles, so much that even his handkerchiefs and apron were used to healed people, who come in contact with it. And in other cases, many people got healed as the shadow of the apostle Peter falls across the sick/
Read: Acts 19:11-12. 5:15-16.

You can walk up and touch the pulpit or platform at the crusade ground, or the robe of the Man of God, or even the chair where he sits, or the car he uses, or anything he comes in contact with; and if you believe it, you'll definitely get healed.

Remember it is not the fringes of the garment of the Man of God that heals you. God says, "...I am The LORD who heals you!"

A Touch from The Healing Hands

Most people believe that they need to be touched by the Man of God or a prophet before they can be healed. This is according to their faith and there is nothing wrong with that. Since you already believe in a special touch from God; let the healing hands touch you. It works wonders. A Man of God filled with the anointing can heal your sicknesses by the laying of the hands on you.

A woman who came for bible study once approached me to

pray for her breast cancer problem. I remember asking her if she believes God can heal her, and she replied with emphatically 'YES!' I prayed for her holding her hands, and about two weeks later she told me the sickness was no longer there as proved by the scan. What a miracle working God!

Let's take a look at some of the events that occurred in the bible times. One day when Jesus arrived at Bethsaida, a group of persons brought him a blind man pleading he should touch him. Responding to them, Jesus took the man outside the village, spat into his eyes, put his hands on him, and ask him, "Do you see anything?" The man looked up and said, "I see people; they look like trees walking around."

Once more Jesus put his hands on the man's eyes. Then his eyes were opened, his sight was restored, and he saw everything clearly/ Read: Mark 8:22-25.

At another time people of various kinds of sicknesses were brought to Jesus. And as he laid his hands on each one, he healed them/ Read: Luke 4:40.

I want you to understand that Jesus acted as a medical doctor at first, when he spat on the blind man's eyes. The blind man didn't see clearly at first. Probably he was seeing things like someone having cataracts. When Jesus asked, he replied and said: "I see men like trees." Then Jesus laid his hands on his eyes again – a second time – a second touch, and his blindness and blurred vision was completely gone!

Sometimes, before Jesus lays his hands on a sick person, he prophesies to the situation. This is what happened on one of the Sabbaths while he was teaching in the temple and a woman crippled by a spirit for eighteen years was there. She was bent over by the sickness and could not be straight.

Imagine how worse her situation was. It's like a young lady of about forty five years walking with a stick like a ninety years old woman. Jesus called her out from the crowd and said to her:

"Woman, you are set free from your infirmity."

Then he put his hands on her, and immediately she straightened up and praised God"/ Read: Luke 13:10-13.

Get Healed By The Spoken Word

If you believe in the power of God upon the Man of God, then you don't need to doubt the Spoken Word Effect.

Now, as you believe in God for your healing and protection, believe also in the Man of God, for he is the angel God will use to bless you. See him as God's messenger filled with the power of God/ Read: 2nd Chronicles 20:20; John 14:1.

God's Word is power; it is Spirit and Life igniting to produce a flow of current like the electrical polarities. Without any limit or boundary, God's word can reach you wherever you are/ Read: John 6:63.

Like rain, once it goes out from the mouth of God through the prophet; it never returns void or without accomplishing that which it was sent forth to do. And because there is power in the tongue, this is the more reason it will work/ Read Isaiah 55:10-11. But I must warn you! The prophet or the Man of God that must minister the Word to you does not necessarily need to be a big prophet that appears on Television or on frontline newspapers.

Do not make this mistake. God can speak through anyone he chooses whether a major or minor prophet, or a brother or sister in the fellowship. All you need to do is pay attention to the word. Test every Spirit. Believe in the prophecy – the word of God, and believe in God/ Read: 1st John 4:1; 1st Thessalonians 5:19-21.

The Man of God who speaks in line with the word of God will cause instant miracles. Anything can happen within this range only if you believe. You don't need a violent or rugged type of prayer before you can get healed. All you need here is faith to demonstrate the spoken word to come into effect and heal you.

A certain commander of the then military regiment had a soldier he loved so much, who was sick and about to die. One day when he heard about Jesus Christ, he sent some elders of the Church to beg Jesus to come and heal his servant. The elders came to Jesus at once and begged him saying, "This man deserve to have you do this, because he loves our nation and has built our synagogue."

Jesus went with them at once to the commander's house. While he was near the house, the centurion sent messengers to him saying, "Lord, don't trouble yourself, for I do not deserve to have you come under my roof. That is why I did not even consider myself worthy to come to you. But say the word, and my servant will be healed."

The commander believes in the power of the spoken word effect. He knows too well that the word of a commander is power. This attitude built a great faith in him, with the understanding that Jesus has even more greater authority in the area of command. Trying to merge the ranks in the place of authority he said through the messengers, "For I myself am a man under authority, with soldiers under me. I tell this one, 'Go,' and he goes; and that one, 'Come,' and he comes. I say to my servant, 'Do this,' and he does it.'"

Jesus was amazed at what the commander had said. And as a result, when the messengers got back home, they found the soldier – the servant of the commander who was sick and near death already healed. / Read: Luke 7:2-10.

He got well by the power of the spoken word effect. The commander only told Jesus, "But say the word, and my servant will be healed."

Do you believe that God's spoken word can heal you right now? The Man of God or the prophet may not need to engage in long prayers before you receive your healing. He just may need to speak the word.

There is a man named Jairus, who was a leader of the synagogue. Jairus was at the crusade ground wanting to invite Jesus to heal his daughter, but while he was waiting there, some men came from his house and said to him, "Your daughter is dead, why border the teacher anymore?"

It is almost hopeless for someone waiting with the doctor to process a medical report for his family member suffering from kidney or liver problem, and the next news that comes to him is "Your daughter or your sister is dead!" This was the situation of Jairus.

While Jairus had already lose hope and is trying to pull himself together, Jesus said to him, "Don't be afraid; just believe." Meanwhile his neighbours began to laugh because they knew it was impossible for anything beyond their imagination to happen. This was because Jesus had earlier said, "The child is not dead, but asleep." But he ignored their mockeries, wailing, and crying.

He took the girl's parents and his closest disciples and went in where the child is. Taking her by the hand, he said, "Talitha Koumi (which means, 'Little girl,

I say to you, 'Get up!'"). Immediately the girl stood up and walked around (She was twelve years old). At this they were completely astonished/ Read: Mark 5:35-42; Luke 5:12-13.

You may be facing a similar situation like Jairus. I want you to know that even when your medical doctor has said there's not going to be a way out.

One word from God can change the situation in your favour. In such a case, you don't depend on the situation you're seeing – you depend on the spoken word of God. If your faith is little, call a Man of God to speak the word. And you can receive your healing even on the phone.

Healing By The Anointing Oil and Prayer

"Is any of you sick? He should call the elders of the church to pray over him and anoint him with oil in the name of the Lord. And the prayer offered in faith will make the sick person well; the Lord will raise him up. If he has sinned he will be forgiven"/
James 5:14-15; Read: Mark 5:13.

So many people have misused the anointing oil. It is very important to note that God's healing power also works with the anointing oil. If you're getting a bottle of the anointing oil (olive oil) as your healing oil; call the elders of the Church to pray over you with the anointing oil. The elders of the church are church leaders and men of great faith. Praying with the anointing oil requires faith to make healing happen. Though, sometimes, sin can become a blockage to prayers.

Have you ever been prayed for by your church elder and still nothing happened? Two things will happen to you when the church elder prays over you and anoint you with oil:

1. The Lord will raise you up

2. Your sins will be forgiving.

With the anointing oil and prayer, you receive both the physical healing of your body and the spiritual healing of your soul, which is your salvation in Christ.

No Sickness is Too Strong for God to Heal

I want you to know that no sickness is too strong or difficult for God to handle. You may have thought it otherwise but that is just the truth.

Is there any sickness tormenting your life right now? You can point a finger to the name of the sickness in the list you may be having, or call the name of that sickness as you hold this book and the healing anointing will flow through your hands. When you have done this, whatever drugs or food you were placed on will begin to work as you take them. Have faith. Everything works when you believe.

Still, you can create an oversight and ask God to heal you from any sickness you're ignorant about. Use the words in the box and make your healing confession now:

> **HEALING CONFESSION**
>
> PRAY NOW: *"O LORD, I know that no sickness is too difficult for you to handle. Please come and heal me from this sickness, in Jesus name. Amen!"*

If you have prayed this prayer and did exactly as instructed, you will feel a moving sensation all over your body. It will become so strong that it might even throw you to the ground. But never mind. God's healing power is at work on your body. And if however nothing happens, it means you will have to read this book all over again from the beginning or play the audio version over and over until your faith is completely built up. Anything can still happen even at night while you are asleep.

You can read it out or play it for someone who is sick, or get someone to read it out for you. Once your faith has grown and saturated, your healing will begin. It doesn't matter if you're already on a medical treatment. Before you made plans to see your medical doctor, God was already dealing with your illnesses. It's all on him whether to heal you by the drugs or heal you as he wishes.

Right now I command you to be healed from every sickness tormenting your life. I command the evil spirit responsible for that disease to leave your body now. I speak peace, relieve, and wellness to every area of your life, business, and soul. I command the powers attacking your health to be drawn in the sea. Let every tablet, balm, injection, food, drugs, or pills you take begin to work with the healing anointing of Jesus Christ. Be healed now in Jesus Christ name. Amen!

Chapter 6: NOW THAT YOU ARE WELL

I have heard people say "My doctor says I shouldn't eat this, I shouldn't eat that, I shouldn't do this, I shouldn't do that." Some people won't even care about the doctor's instructions. They would simply say "That's his business; I eat what I want to, and I do what I want to do."

It is always possible for sick patients to forget doctor's instructions on nutrition and healthy lifestyles, after recovering from their illnesses.

Jesus Christ said to the man who was healed from a protracted sickness of thirty eight years, "See, you are well again. Stop sinning or something worse may happen to you"/ John 5:14. Whenever you go against a professional instruction of your healthy living, you are bound to suffer from the same sickness or even a more complicated type. The simple instruction is now that you are well, stay away from anything that fights against your freedom of living.

If the doctor says stopping smoking of cigarette and other hard drug will help you get back your life just do it. You might have had a second chance; but you may not have a second life.

God wants you to stay alive and be in health.

Follow the preacher's instructions from the Holy Book and you'll live a long and fulfilled life. It works. Why not give it a try?

Learn To Appreciate

Most people do not see gratitude to God as important. They just think that paying their hospital bills is all that matters. But it is good to note that before the medical doctor is able to certify that you are completely well, God was already working on your body. This means that God already dealt with the root of your sickness before the tablets or injections were able to wwork well on your body.

There are also some people who, after series of treatments, still cannot get better. Not that the doctors were not professionals. God sometimes allow this to happen so you could look up to him for your healing and be appreciative. Talking about appreciation to God; it can speed up a healing process and keep you immune from every sickness attack.

An appreciation is usually giving the best of your gifts to the Church or to the Man of God, and a confession of healing that goes like this: "Thank you Lord for healing me!" Learn to do it as a daily duty to appreciate God for your health. Thank him for every part of you that is functioning even if some part of your body might be sick.

It is possible that you might still have pains or some signs that appears as though the sickness is still there. Don't wait until you're perfectly healed before you make these sacrifices. God wants to see how thankful you can be/ Read: Luke 5:14.

A certain time in the bible history, ten lepers stood at a distance shouting with a loud voice: "...Jesus, Master, have pity on us."

When he saw them, he said,

"Go, show yourselves to the priests."

And as they went, they were cleansed.' One of them, when he saw he was healed, came back, praising God in a loud voice. He threw himself at Jesus' feet and thanked him – and he was a Samaritan.'

Jesus asked, 'Were not all ten cleansed? Where are the other nine? 'Was no one found to return and give praise to God except this foreigner?' Then he said to him,

"Rise and go; your faith has made you well"'/ Luke 17:12-19. The last words Jesus said to the leper are the kind of words every sick person or patient is expecting from his doctor.

These ten lepers got healed on their way after Jesus told them to go to the Church and let the pastor or the Man of God carry out a check of their testimony claim. But they all went their way refusing to show this gratitude. However one of them who came back and said, "Thank you Jesus for healing me," was perfectly healed.

And what do you think of the other nine lepers? Will they be perfectly healed for refusing to appreciate the one who healed them? Of course not! The reason is the healing is tied to appreciation. You need to follow a simple instruction, "Go, show yourselves to the priests."

It means make yourself known to the Man of God that you have been healed, and that there may be a public testimony of your healing to the glory of God. That's exactly what Jesus said to the lepers/ Read: Luke 5:14.

Don't hide a testimony of your healing like the other nine lepers. If you do, your sickness may return. Testify it; and let men know you have been healed by the power of God. Remember, the leper who came back to thank God, was the one who had his healing retained. Being ungrateful can make you lose everything you have. Now that you are well, learn to appreciate God for your new health condition. Why not begin now!

Like the ten lepers, so many people have been healed by faith unknowing to them. Their healing is manifested when they confess and show gratitude to God. Confess your healing as many times as you can. As you do, Jesus is saying to you, "Rise and go; your faith has made you well." The more you confess and appreciate God, the healthier you become. You can say it out like this:

"Thank you Jesus, I am healed! Thank you Lord, I am healed! Thank you Jesus, I am healed!

And remember this, there are so many times you have contacted one sickness or the other. It ate deep into you and you lived with it in your ignorance. All those times God gave you a special grace and the sickness didn't blow you up. You know why? God wanted to let you know that he's the Lord who heals you.

Now you understand why you should appreciate God for your health and make a constant confession of your healing by the power of God.

But what will happen if you refuse to appreciate God after you have been healed? The answer is nothing that you already know. And if you actually choose to be an ingrate, you will be provoking God to anger. Guess what happen next when God is angry at you?

Here is the like of the situation with King Hezekiah, who was cured of strange boils and had another fifteen years added to his limping life.

In spite of this great miracle God did, Hezekiah didn't show gratitude to God, and God was very angry both at him and all the people under his government.

Somehow King Hezekiah realized he had not thanked God for his healing upon his life. At this repentance, God changed his mind and averted his wrath from him and the entire occupants of the land where he governs.

So everyone was safe because of the King's thanksgiving service/ Read: 2nd Chronicles 32:24-28.

Confess Your Sins To Each Other

There are sicknesses that will never be healed until a confession of sin has been made. So many people have had their miracles delayed as a result of hiding their sins. They've attended several crusade and church meetings and yet their conditions have remained the same. The bible says, "Therefore confess your sins to each other and pray for each other so that you may be

healed. The prayer of a righteous man is powerful and effective..."/
James 5:16-17.

Now that you have known the truth, you are already well by faith. Do you want to see your healing manifest? The best thing to do now is to stop hiding your sins. God wants to free you from that bondage. Confess them to someone who is ready to pray for you and your healing will be manifested.

Watch What You Eat and Do

The life you live on daily bases worth placing on a check. If you however will forget to do it, ask a responsible friend to keep watch on you. It may actually seem hard to follow through, but once you face it squarely it'll begin to make sense.

Remember the saying, "You can't eat your cake and have it." Sometimes, when you feel you're okay with bobbling, life will always have a way of proving you wrong.

The Good Book has a strong defense on this philosophy. It clarifies that "There is a way that seem right to a man, but in the end it leads to death"/ Proverbs 14:12.

Watch what you eat and do. They are likely to have a very stronghold on your life. Every time you eat, drink, or do anything to make your moment, you are, at that time adding to your life or subtracting from your life. This is a clear fact that certain foods may not be helpful at some point of your life/ Read: Judges 13:4,13,14.

Always feel free to make changes whenever you're no longer comfortable. Changing of diet can help give you a new look. Don't waste your energy trying to please people when you're always uncomfortable with the way you live. It's your life, not theirs.

Get a pastor for yourself, and get a medical doctor as well as a nutritionist. Follow these professional guides I have listed on the next page to keep your entire life healthy. :

Keep your life on a regular check.

Always remember that you have just one life.

Avoid careless and unhygienic lifestyles.

Choose your friends or associates if you like.

Never let anyone influence your life with those things you no longer practice.

Be conscious of the rampant reoccurring presence of sicknesses.

Learn how to listen to helpful health tips and put them in practice.

Try to understand the state of your health and visit your doctor or prophet where necessary.

Wriggle your body at list 15 minutes daily with useful exercise to keep you strong and free from any illness.

Learn to watch comic shows or get people to make you laugh.

Laughter is good for your spirit, soul and body health. It's a natural medicine that has a way of changing bad moods.

Chapter 7: GET SAVED AND LIVE HAPPILY

Salvation is a free gift to every man. God wants you to be saved and live happily. You may have received a healing from God when you were never saved even while you are a church member; I want you to know that not all who goes to church are saved. Being saved means you're exempted from judgment. And the only answer to this way of salvation is to accept the man called Jesus Christ into your life. The Good Book says, "Salvation is found in no one else, for there is no other name under heaven given to men by which we must be saved"/ Acts 4:12.

A saved person is a happy person. No matter your achievements in life; you cannot find true happiness unless you have gotten salvation in Christ. Give your life completely to Jesus and he'll secure everything you have.

But why do you need to accept Jesus Christ before you're saved? The reason is Jesus is the free gift God gave to the fallen world to restore the fortunes of men. God had a Son, who was begotten, not of the way of men, but by the way of the Spirit. This man called Jesus is the Word, which comes out from the mouth of God. And now it pleases God to use this same Word, which created everything that be, to be human – in flesh and blood, as The Saviour/ Read: John 1:1-14.

It was written a long time ago: "For God so loved the world, that he gave his only begotten Son, that whosoever believeth in him should not perish, but have everlasting life – *KJV*. For God did not send his Son into the world to condemn the world, but to save the world through him – *NIV*.

"He that believeth on him is not condemned: but he that believeth not is condemned already, because he hath not believed in the name of the only begotten Son of God – *KJV*"/ John 3:16-18.

First, you have to begin by confessing him with your mouth, and then, believe him in your heart. As the scriptures say: "That if you confess with your mouth, 'Jesus is Lord,' and believe in your heart that God raised him from the dead, you will be saved. For it is with your heart that you believe and are justified, and it is with your mouth that you confess and are saved"/ Romans 10:9-10.

This salvation means you cannot go back to do the evil things you used to do. Your life has come to a turning point as you made those confessions and you are now different. You are born of God, and anyone who is born of God cannot sin. His life is hidden from the evil one because he believes in the only Son of God/ Read: 1ˢᵗ John 5:18-20. Sin, as you now know is a virus that inflicts you with sickness.

Staying free from sickness is possible. After you have gotten saved by those confessions, do these and you'll live a happy life in Jesus Christ:

- ✓ Keep your body, mind, and soul in tune with the Spirit of God.

- ✓ Do not live anymore

like you used to.

- ✓ Go to a Church that preaches the hard truth, but be a light everywhere you go.

- ✓ Read your bible as often as possible and meditate on what you read.

- ✓ Pray always in the Spirit for everyone and those experiencing your kind of trouble.

- ✓ Love your enemies and forgive those who have wronged you badly.

- ✓ Endure suffering as a Christian

and trust that God is always with you to take you out of trouble.

- ✓ Help people who are in need whenever you are in position to help.

- ✓ Pay your Tithes and Offering and give support to the work of God

- ✓ Never give in to temptation because the devil is still prowling around like a roaring lion.

And finally do not forget this promise. God says, "If you listen carefully to the voice of the LORD your God and do what is right in his eyes, if you pay attention to his commands and keep all his decrees, I will not bring on you any of the diseases I brought on the Egyptians, for *I*

am the LORD, who heals you."/
Exodus 15:26.

READ OTHER BOOKS BY BRAVE MIC

BEST SELLER LEADERSHIP / PHILOSOPHY SERIES

1. FAITHFUL COLONELS
2. THE 84 LAWS OF FURTUNE AND MISFURTUNE vol.1-4
3. THE REAL EXTRAORDINARY MAN
4. POWER DRUNK POLITICS

SUCCESS / WINNING SERIES

5. SUCCESS GODDESS vol.1-2
6. SEVEN SUCCESS ENEMIES YOU MUST OVERCOME
7. WHY YOU'RE OFTEN NOT FINISHING WELL
8. FIVE SECRETS TO DISCOVERING YOUR NICHE
9. YOU CAN RISE TO THE PEAK

10. THE SECRETS OF GREATNESS

11. BEYOND LIMITATION

12. SUCCEEDING WITHOUT PENNY

13. THE DEVIL DOES NOT EXIST

14. YOU'RE NOT A FAILURE UNTIL YOU QUIT

15. DOUBTS

HEALTH, HEALING / DELIVERANCE SERIES

16. DEAD BONES

17. I AM THE LORD WHO HEALS YOU

18. CUTTTING THE GORDIAN KNOT

19. GETTING HEALED FROM DEMONIC TORMENT

20. STAYING FREE FROM WORRRIES

21. SUICIDE SPIRIT RELEAVER

22. STABILIZING YOUR CRITICAL SITUATION

23. FIXING EMOTIONAL RENT

24. IN THE NAME OF JESUS

SELF DISCOVERY / IMPROVEMENT SERIES

25. YOU'RE NOT CREATED POOR

26. UNDERSTANDING AND FULFILLING YOUR CALLING

27. FETCH THE WATER WITH THE MUCK

28. GREAT POTENTIALS

29. THE VAGABOND RESOURCE

30. TREASURE IN THE DESERT

31. LIFE STEP UP STRATEGIES

THE FIGHTING MAN SERIES

32. YEILDING TO TEMPTATION AND THE WAY OUT

33. THE EVIL STRATEGIST

34. YOU CAN WIN EVERY BATTLE

35. TREAD THOSE POWERS UNDER YOUR FEET

36. STANDING TALL IN TIMES OF PRESSURES

37. DEALING WITH OBSTACLES

38. SPIRIT COUNTERFORCE

39. A TRUE SOLDIER

SPIRITUAL SCIENCE SERIES

40. WORTHY ADVERSARIES IN THE WORLD OF DIPLOMATIC DEMONS

FAITH EXPLOIT SERIES

41. THE EIGHT WONDERS OF FAITH

42. SIX EXTRAODINARY THINGS YOUR TINGUE CAN DO

43. THE FORCEFUL NATURE OF YOUR MIND

44. WHEN THE BROOK DRIES UP

MARRIAGE / LOVE SCIENCE SERIES

45. BEFORE YOU MAKE THAT WISH

46. THE RIGHT MARRIAGE PARTNER

47. MARRIAGE ISSUES

48. THE GODLY QUEEN

49. SYSTEMATIC RELATIONSHIP

THE MAKING OF THE MAN SERIES

50. LIVING ABOVE BANKRUPTCY

51. AFFLICTION

52. FOURTEEN YEARS IN THE BELLY OF THE FISH

53. LIVING FOR A PURPOSE

54. CUT DOWN BUT NOT DESTROYED

55. HUMILIATED FOR GLORY

56. GOD'S PLAN B

THE SOUL WINNING PROGRAMME SERIES

57. ENJOYING LIFE WITHOUT TEAR

58. I AM YOUR SAVIOUR

59. THE ULTIMATE MISSION

60. RUGGED EVANGELSM

61. LOVE HAS NO ENEMY

TIME IS RUNNING OUT BROADCASTER SERIES

62. SEASON 1 – 9

WALKING IN THE SPIRIT SERIES

63. THE PERSON OF THE HOLY SPIRIT

64. GOD IS STILL SPEAKING

65. WHEN THE SPIRIT MOVES

66. SPIRITUAL HYGENIC PRINCIPLES

67. ONE SPARK IS ENOUGH

68. THE NOISE AND THE VOICE

ATTITUDE MANAGEMENT SERIES

69. HOW TO HANDLE YOUR TEMPERAMENT

70. THE ANTIDOTE FOR SEXUAL OFFENCES

71. THE WAYWARD WIFE

72. ONE LITTLE MISTAKE

73. VICTIMIZED

74. YOU BROKE IT YOU FIX IT

MAKING THINGS HAPPEN SERIES

75. THE PERSISTENT SPIRIT

76. TURNING OPORTUNITIES INTO PROFITING DEAL

77. BREAKING OUT OF CIRCLES

78. WALKING IN THE REALM OF POSSIBILITY

79. OVERCOMING THE ENEMY CALLED FEAR

80. MAKE THAT MOVE

GENUINE WEALTH INVESTMENT SERIES

81. BREAKING THROUGH FINANCIAL OBSTACLES

82. WHEN MONEY DOESN'T MAKE SENSE

83. JUDAS ISCARIOT IN THE CHURCH

EFFECTIVE PRAYERS SERIES

84. TEN WAYS TO EFFECTIVE SPIRITUAL COMMUNICATION

85. LORD, TEACH US HOW TO PRAY

HEAVEN BOUND SERIES

86. WEARING THE BADGE OF A TRUE BELIEVER

87. GROWING INTO PERFECTION IN CHRIST

88. SERVING GOD FAITHFULLY IN EVERY SITUATION

89. LIFE AT THE AFTERLIFE

THE AUTHOR

Dr. Brave Mic is an International Teacher, Tele-evangelist, Healing Pastor, Author of over 88 bestselling books in 18 life changing series and President of Salvation Miracles Embassy Inc.

He is a gifted speaker in government and leadership of all walks of life. Not only has he opened the eyes of many to see the truth; there have been proves of healings and miracles since December 11, 88.

As Spiritual Scientist and Teacher of Human Sciences, his quest is to demonstrate love through lives saving and souls saving, and at the same time transform minds from the world's biggest mistake and ignorance.

FACEBOOK
Connect with Dr. Brave Mic on this Facebook pages:
- Salvation Miracles Embassy
- Brave Mic Ministries
- Time Is Running Out Broadcast with Brave Mic

YOUTUBE TV CHANNEL
Watch Brave Mic on this YouTube TV Channel: TMTN UNIVERSAL or use the link:
https://www.youtube.com/channel/UCC7RfzjamjCZGF_djx1drEQ

ABOUT THE BOOK

The world's biggest setback is the creating of many problems and having just a few solutions. Discoveries also have proved that in accounting for life's pitfall, so many unknown dangerous aliens have shown to be responsible for bad health and untimely deaths. Every second that passes we see people suffer unjustly and die mysteriously; proving the fact that the world itself and everyone claiming to exist is sick. All these have resulted from the lack of knowledge according to God's instructions and it's violations.

I AM THE LORD WHO HEALS YOU, is a book for the total health of the sick, inspired to crush the malignant enemy and his wide-spread plague – the threat that poses from sin to disease attacks, and at the same time alleviate the sickly pains inflicted on the entire human race. It brings you to the world's biggest clinic with the Great Physician, and then teaches you how to confront your bad health situation, plus the secret of living a long and happy life.

In this book, beyond the ordinary and scientific knowledge, Dr. Brave Mic have exposed causes of total health attack and prescribed ways in which you can get healed and stay healthy in spirit, soul and body. Did you know that every sickness has a cure if we are able to discover it? Read this book and you'll find all the solutions to your health problems in here. Remember, the Great Physician is the last medical scientist you need today. With him, believe it, your problem is solved!

Made in United States
North Haven, CT
08 June 2025